Name the Seven Dwarfs

Name
THE SEVEN DWARFS
and
OTHER NUMBERED
DIVERSIONS

Diane Giddis

WILLIAM MORROW AND COMPANY, INC.
New York

Library of Congress Cataloging-in-Publication Data

Giddis, Diane.
    Name the seven dwarfs and other numbered diversions / Diane
Giddis.
        p.   cm.
    ISBN: 0-688-09388-4
    1. Questions and answers.   I. Title.
AG   195.G48   1990
031—dc20   90-8083
                                                       CIP

Printed in the United States of America

First Edition

1   2   3   4   5   6   7   8   9   10

BOOK DESIGN BY PAUL CHEVANNES

To my mother, Rolande:
Let me count the ways

Acknowledgments

Thanks beyond number to: my editor, Randy Ladenheim-Gil, for helping transform a beer-fueled notion into a bona fide book; Jim Trupin, a gent and a wit as well as a skillful and savvy agent; David Grambs, always there with invaluable support, inordinate smarts, and innumerable suggestions; Ryan Anthony, Kathryn Lance, and her parents, John and Kathryn, whose contributions, both in number and importance, I'm still trying to calculate; and The New York Public Library, especially the Jefferson Market branch and its wonderfully helpful staff (special mention to Paul Schmidt). And to Steve Weller, who provided the initial inspiration.

Introduction

One night in a bar about a twelvemonth ago, I made a casual reference to the eternal verities, probably to fill a gap in the conversation. My companion nodded. There was a pause. "What are the eternal verities, anyway?" he finally asked.

"You mean you don't know?" I answered, quickly adding, "How are you on the seven dwarfs?"

As it turned out, he was a little stronger on the seven dwarfs than I was on the eternal verities, my knowledge of which was confined to a dimly remembered reference in William Faulkner's Nobel Prize acceptance speech. (And I didn't get even that right: Faulkner spoke of the *old* verities, "the old universal truths.") Even now, having reread the speech, I'm not sure I could safely identify the verities, eternal or old, with any precision (I think they're love and honor and pity and pride and compassion and sacrifice, but courage and hope may be in there, too). I can, however, definitely name all seven dwarfs, as well as the seven deadly sins, the Four Horsemen of the Apocalypse, the nine Muses, the twelve Apostles, the nine circles of Hell, the Four Freedoms, the five W's of journalism, and about 250 other numbered phenomena. For—as so often happens when you're just sitting around blithely pursuing some inconsequential business—that night an idea for a book was born. A book about things—items, persons, groups, constellations—with numbers attached to them.

Fortunately for the future of that idea, the number—as it were—of those things turned out to be surprisingly large. Maybe because by enumerating, organizing, and classifying the things of this world, humans can feel they're exercising some sort of control over them. Leaders, especially, seem prone to making lists. Franklin Roosevelt proclaimed the Four Freedoms; Woodrow Wilson, the Fourteen Points; Buddha, the Four Noble Truths; and let's not forget the Bill of Rights, the first ten amendments to the Constitution— the work of some big-time leaders. Even the Almighty wasn't immune, according to Moses, Maimonides, and Matthew, Mark, et al.: hence we have the Ten Commandments and the Thirteen Articles of Faith and the Twelve Tribes of Israel and the Eight Beatitudes and— well, many other divinely designated categories.

The months I spent compiling these lists should have enabled me to draw many sage conclusions about numbers and groupings and the ramifications and significance thereof, but ultimately my reflections boil down, essentially, to three:

(1) Everybody loves numbered categories—Christians, Jews, Buddhists, Hindus, Muslims, pagans (Greeks and Romans), Chinese, Japanese, and the Norse. The impulse to identify things by number as well as by name seems well-nigh universal, not to mention eternal.

(2) Unlike the East, Near or Far, the West has a pronounced tendency—if not a compulsive need—to compile top-ten lists: witness the David Letterman show and

the FBI's Ten Most Wanted and the weekly box-office listings and the Nielsen ratings and all the pop-culture critics at the end of the year. There may be some profound, if vague, connection here to the Ten Commandments (the first top-ten list), though it would take someone far more sacrilegious than I to come up with it.

(3) Top-ten lists aside, the most popular number, at least as far as this book is concerned, is 3. There are at least three times as many entries in the 3's as in any other number category, and a lot more could have been included. Given that the world in general, at least ideally, tends to be divided into couples—taking its cue, perhaps, from Adam and Eve, or the first gene division—it's worth noting that so many of its phenomena seem to group themselves into threes. Divinities, against all logic, are often composed of threes, and there are far more nameable trios of every kind than duos, quartets, and quintets. There are three Witches, three Magi, three Furies, three Graces, three Musketeers, three Stooges, three Little Pigs, and of course we tend to see everything in terms of a beginning, a middle, and an end. Most plays, if not lives, have three acts, and there is no such thing (except in this book) as a list of two. Maybe we just don't get a sense of *number* until we reach three, and once we hit it feel a bit tired and decide we can rest. Whatever the reason, it's clear that 3 is the number humanity finds most satisfying—at least as a number.

Finally, a note on How to Use This Book. It can be used in two—possibly three—ways:

(1) As a straight quiz book. You can read the question (or heading), try to list the answers, and then look them up to see how you did. Unfortunately, if you go

for broke, you're likely to find this method frustrating, since most readers probably won't be able to list all of the answers to most of the questions, especially as they climb up the numerical ladder.

(2) As a handy reference work. A highly recommended method, particularly if you tend to be a sore loser. Think of this as a Cultural Literacy quiz (sometimes wedded to Trivial Pursuit) in which you're not expected to know the answers—just to be interested in them. Here are the answers to all—well, some—of the questions you've always wondered about but never dared to ask (for fear of exposing your ignorance). And even some you never thought to ask.

(3) As a combination of the two. Most people can name five, at best six, dwarfs; three, at best four, Wonders of the World. Maybe a couple of amendments; if Christian, four or five Apostles. Given that, let's see how many items you can come up with on any list you choose to take on, then fill in the blanks of your cultural knowledge.

Or, to put it another way, think of this as the ultimate bar-bet book, the settler of all those bedeviling questions that have a multipart answer. ("What are you, crazy? Dizzy wasn't no dwarf." "Covetousness—isn't that the same as envy?" "Yeah—well, what about Shemp?") Which is, more or less, where we came in.

Questions

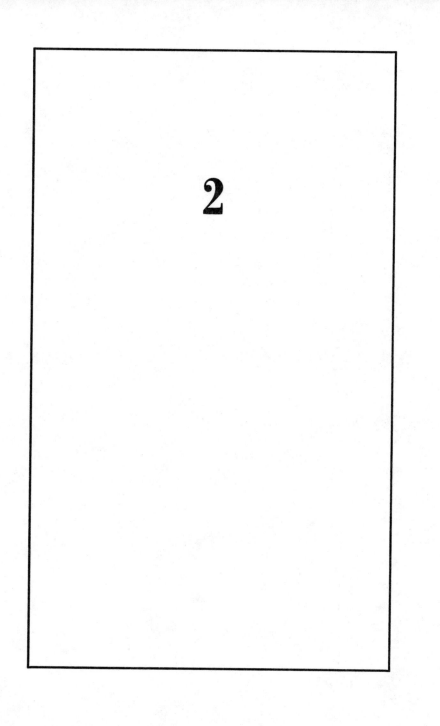

2

1 | THE TWO GENTLEMEN OF VERONA

2 | The Two PILLARS OF HERCULES

3 | THE TWIN CITIES

4 | The Actors Who Played TWO FOR THE ROAD

5 | The Twins Who Represent GEMINI

6 | THE DIOSCURI

7 | THE TWO NOBLE KINSMEN

8 | The DYNAMIC DUO

9 | DUAL MONARCHY

10 | THE ODD COUPLE
And the Performers Who Played Them

11 | THE TWO HEMISPHERES OF THE GLOBE

12 | THE TWO HEMISPHERES OF THE CEREBRUM

13 | THE "ORIGINAL" SIAMESE TWINS

14 | The Actors Who Played TWINS

18

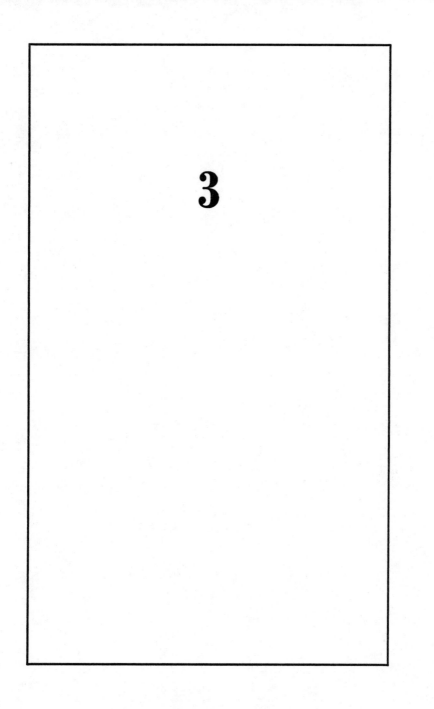

3

52 | THE Three CHIPMUNKS

53 | THREE KINGDOMS (Chinese History)

54 | THE THREE KINGDOMS OF NATURE

55 | John Dos Passos' *U.S.A.* Trilogy

56 | The Member Nations of the TRIPLE ENTENTE (1907)

57 | THE THREE CABALLEROS

58 | MY THREE SONS

59 | The THREE ESTATES in France and England

60 | THE Three BRONTË SISTERS

61 | The Three Categories of the TRIAD (Military Weapons)

62 | THE THREE THEOLOGICAL VIRTUES

63 | The Three M's in the 3M COMPANY

64 | THE Three ANDREWS SISTERS

65 | The Three Events in a TRIATHLON

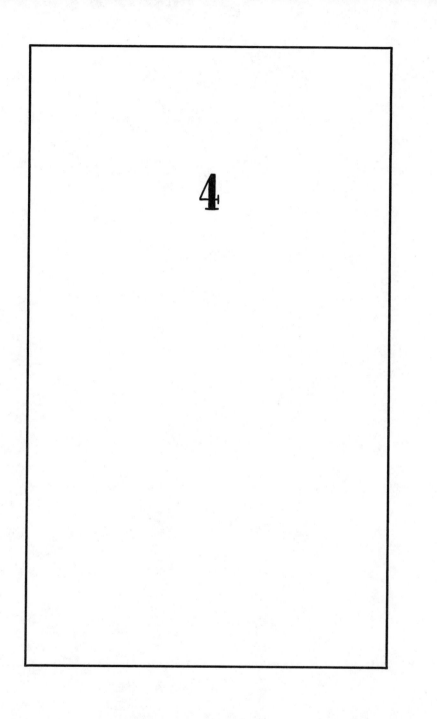

4

121 | **THE FOUR CARDINAL or NATURAL VIRTUES**

122 | **The Four Powers of the FOUR-POWER PACT or TREATY**

123 | **The FOUR AGES of Humankind**

124 | *Ordinal*

THE FOURTH ESTATE

125 | *Ordinal*

The FOURTH MAN of the Soviet Spy Ring in Britain

5

34

6

7

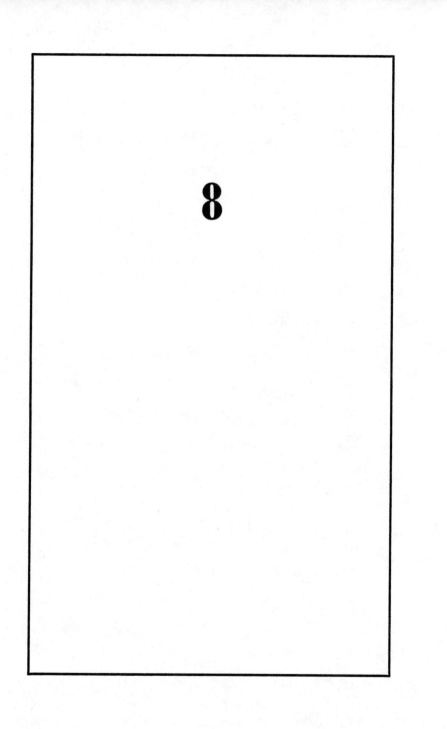

8

9

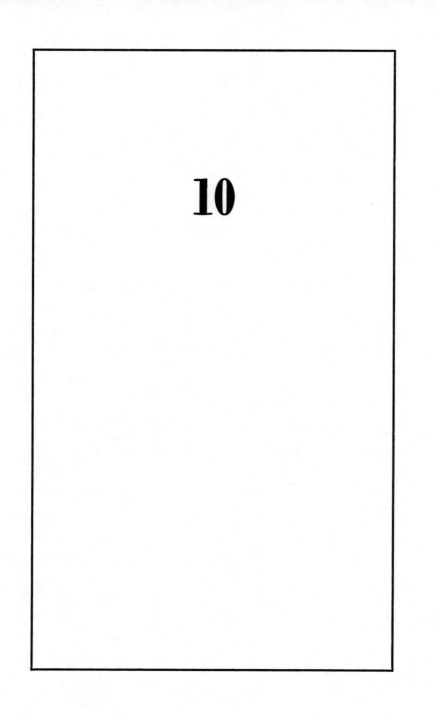

10

58

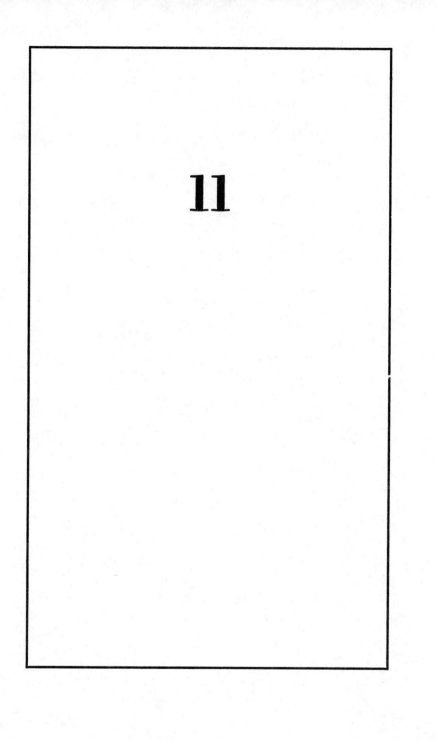

11

235 | **The Actors Who Played OCEAN'S ELEVEN**

236 | **THE ELEVEN STATES OF THE CONFEDERACY**

12

249 | **THE TWELVE GODS ON MOUNT OLYMPUS**

250 | **The Actors Who Played 12 ANGRY MEN**

251 | **THE TWELVE (Minor) PROPHETS**

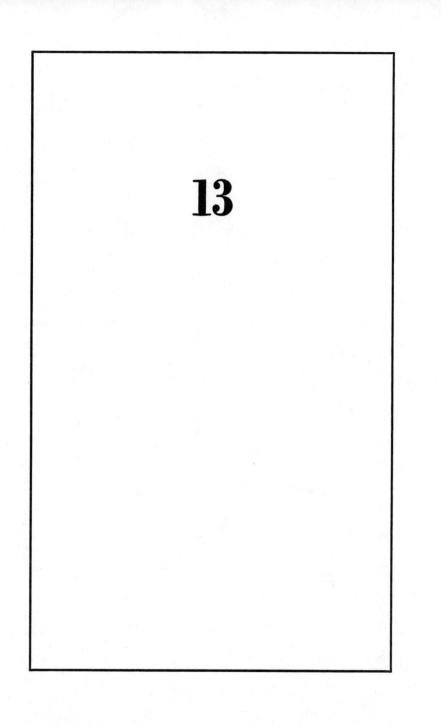

13

14

Answers

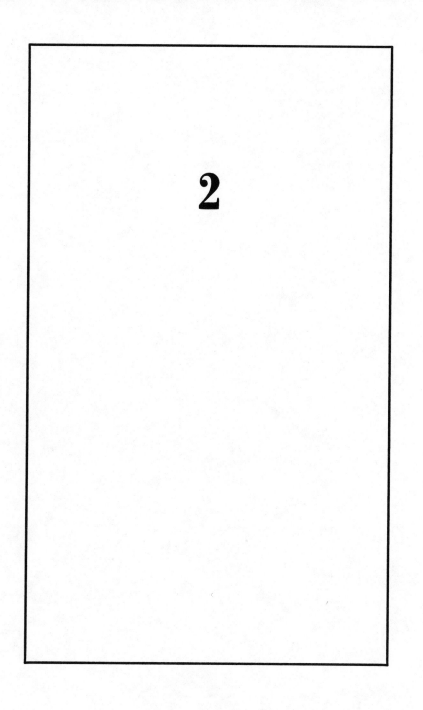

2

1 | Valentine and Proteus were the gents in Shakespeare's *The Two Gentlemen of Verona* (c.1594).

2 | The promontories at the eastern end of the Strait of Gibraltar: the Rock of Gibraltar in Europe and Jebel Musa at Ceuta in Africa. They were anciently called Calpe and Abyla. (See *The Twelve Labors of Heracles*, page 161.)

3 | Minneapolis and St. Paul (Minnesota).

4 | Audrey Hepburn and Albert Finney were the married couple in the 1967 movie *Two for the Road.*

5 | Castor and Pollux. Castor (Alpha Geminorum) and Pollux (Beta Geminorum) are the two brightest stars in the constellation.

6 | Castor and Pollux (or Polydeuces), twin deities who were the sons of Leda and either Zeus, the king of the gods, or Tyndareus, Leda's husband.

7 | Palamon and Arcite are the titular characters in *The Two Noble Kinsmen* (written c. 1613 and published in 1634), which is believed to be a collaboration between John Fletcher and Will Shakespeare.

8 | Batman and Robin.

9 | The joint kingdom of Austria-Hungary, which was established in 1867 under Emperor Francis Joseph and came to an end in 1918.

10 | Oscar Madison and Felix Unger.

Walter Matthau and Art Carney originated the roles of Oscar and Felix on Broadway in 1965. Matthau (Oscar) and Jack Lemmon (Felix) played them in the 1968 movie. The TV series starring Jack Klugman as Oscar and Tony Randall as Felix ran from 1970 to 1975. In 1982, Oscar and Felix returned to television as *The New Odd Couple,* with Demond Wilson and Ron Glass in the roles, but the show lasted only one season.

11 | There are two sets of hemispheres: Northern and Southern, Eastern and Western. The Northern Hemisphere consists of that half of the earth between the North Pole and the Equator; the Southern, between the South Pole and the Equator. The Eastern Hemisphere consists of Europe, Africa, Asia, and Australia; the Western, of North and South America, the surrounding waters, and the neighboring islands.

12 | The left and right hemispheres (also called the left brain and the right brain). The left hemisphere generally controls the right side of the body and such functions as speech, writing, and calculation, while the right hemisphere controls the left side and such functions as spatial perception.

13 | Chang and Eng, born in 1811 of Chinese parents in Siam, today Thailand. (They died in 1874 at the age of 62.)

14 | Danny DeVito and Arnold Schwarzenegger were the title characters in *Twins* (1988).

15 | Ann and Alice were the first names of the two
Mrs. Grenvilles in Dominick Dunne's 1985 novel
of that name, later made into a TV movie with Ann-
Margret as Ann and Claudette Colbert as Alice.

16 | Six-year-old Freddie and Flossie and twelve-year-
old Bert and Nan.

17 | Tropic of Cancer; Tropic of Capricorn. These two
boundaries of the Torrid Zone are, respectively,
about 23½ degrees north and 23½ degrees south of
the Equator.

18 | Paul Reiser (Michael Taylor) and Greg Evigan (Joey
Harris) played the fathers in the television series
My Two Dads.

19 | World War I: 1914–18 (more specifically, July 28,
1914–November 11, 1918).

World War II: 1939–45 (Germany invaded Poland on
September 1, 1939, and surrendered to the Allies on
May 8, 1845; Japan surrendered on August 14, 1945).

20 | Henry Fonda and Anne Bancroft played the cou-
ple in *Two for the Seesaw* on Broadway in 1958;
Robert Mitchum and Shirley MacLaine in the 1962
movie.

21 | The terrible twins Hans and Fritz, created in 1897,
wreaked their havoc in animated cartoons and a
syndicated comic strip for decades.

22 | Alexandre Dumas *père* named his *frères Corses* Lucien de Franchi (the sporty one) and Louis de Franchi (the scholarly one).

23 | Bill Medley and Bobby Hatfield were the white soul singers popular in the sixties. (They were soul, not blood, brothers.)

24 | Chicago. (New York is the first.)

3

25 | Athos, Porthos, and Aramis were the three title characters in Alexandre Dumas *père*'s 1844 novel, *The Three Musketeers.*

26 | In the 1948 film version of *The Three Musketeers,* Van Heflin played Athos; Gig Young, Porthos; and Robert Coote, Aramis. (Gene Kelly was D'Artagnan.) In the 1974 version, Oliver Reed was Athos; Frank Finlay, Porthos; and Richard Chamberlain, Aramis.

27 | Moe (Howard), Larry (Fine), and Curly (Howard). After Curly (né Jerome) left the team in 1946, he was replaced by, in succession, Shemp Howard (who was part of the original act until 1930), Joe Besser, and Joe DeRita ("Curly Joe").

28 | Olga, Masha, and Irina were the three Prozorov sisters in Anton Chekhov's 1901 drama, *The Three Sisters.*

29 | Melchior (who offered gold), Gaspar or Caspar (frankincense), and Balthazar (myrrh).

30 | Known as the *Gratiae* to the Romans and the *Charites* to the Greeks, these goddesses of charm and beauty were called Aglaia (Brilliance or Brightness), Thalia (Bloom or Flowering), and Euphrosyne (Joy).

31 | The three goddesses of destiny (*Moirai* to the Greeks; *Fata* or *Parcae* to the Romans) were Clotho, who spun the thread of life; Lachesis, who held it and determined its length; and Atropos, who cut it off. Their Roman names were Nona, Decuma, and Morta.

32 These three goddesses of vengeance (*Erinyes* or *Eumenides* to the Greeks; *Furiae* to the Romans) were named Tisiphone (Avenger), Alecto (Unceasing), and Megaera (Jealous).

33 Eve White, Eve Black, and Jane were the names of the three personae of the famous multiple personality, portrayed by Joanne Woodward in the 1957 film *The Three Faces of Eve*.

34 Reading, 'riting, and 'rithmetic.

35 The three components of Buddhism are the Buddha himself; the *dharma,* or *dhamma* (doctrine, or law); and the *sangha* (monastic order, or community of monks).

36 *The Fellowship of the Ring* (1954), *The Two Towers* (1955), and *The Return of the King* (1956) are the three books in J. R. R. Tolkien's saga.

37 The Allied leaders who met at Yalta in February 1945 to plan the end of the war, the disposition of Germany, the fate of Poland, and other matters were Franklin D. Roosevelt, Winston Churchill, and Joseph Stalin.

38 Ford Motor Company, Chrysler Corporation, and General Motors Corporation.

39 The Father, the Son, and the Holy Ghost, or Holy Spirit.

40 In the United States, the Kentucky Derby at Churchill Downs, Kentucky; the Preakness Stakes at Pimlico, Maryland; and the Belmont Stakes at Belmont Park, New York. In England, the Two Thousand Guineas at Newmarket; the Derby at Epsom Downs; and the Saint Leger at Doncaster.

41 | At the end of the season, the player who leads his league in batting average, home runs, and RBIs (runs batted in).

42 | Unity of action, unity of time, and unity of place (as set forth in Aristotle's *Poetics*).

43 | Snap, Crackle, and Pop.

44 | The three soldiers of Rudyard Kipling's volume of short stories, *Soldiers Three,* are Otheris, Learoyd, and Mulvaney. (They previously appeared in *Plain Tales from the Hills.*)

45 | There were actually three Triple Alliances:

(1) an alliance among England, Sweden, and the Dutch Republic against France in 1668; (2) an alliance among Great Britain, France, and the Dutch Republic against Spain in 1717; (3) an alliance between Germany and Austria-Hungary in 1879, which Italy joined in 1882 and which lasted until Italy entered World War I in 1915.

46 | The Bronx, Manhattan, and Queens.

47 | Pompey, Caesar, and Crassus made up the First Triumvirate (60 B.C.); Mark Antony, Lepidus, and Octavian (Augustus), the Second (43 B.C.).

48 | Height, width, and depth.

49 | Sun Yat-sen articulated these three influential Communist principles in 1924:

1. Nationalism, or self-determination for the Chinese.
2. Democracy, or the rights of the people, with the actual government in the hands of a qualified elite representing the masses.
3. "People's Livelihood," or equalization of land ownership.

50 | Red, blue, and yellow.

51 | This trinity is composed of Brahmā, the Creator; Vishnu (or Visnu), the Preserver; and Shiva (or Siva), the Destroyer.

52 | Alvin, Simon, and Theodore are the names of the singing cartoon characters.

53 | The three states into which China was divided from A.D. 220 to 280 were the Wei, the Shu Han, and the Wu. The period of the Three Kingdoms has been the subject of many legends and literary works.

54 | Animal, vegetable, and mineral.

55 | *The 42nd Parallel* (1930), *1919* (1932), and *The Big Money* (1936).

56 | Great Britain, France, and Russia, the nucleus of the Allies in World War I.

57 | Donald Duck, Joe Carioca, and Panchito were the trio cavorting through Latin America in the 1945 feature-length cartoon (with live action) of the same title.

58 | Steve Douglas's (Fred MacMurray's) three sons in the long-running sitcom were Mike (Tim Considine), Robbie (Don Grady), and Chip (Stanley Livingston). After Mike got married and moved East, Steve adopted the orphaned Ernie (Barry Livingston).

59 | The Estates General (*États généraux*) in France before the Revolution consisted of the clergy, the nobles, and the commons. In Great Britain the three estates of the realm are the Lords Spiritual and the Lords Temporal (forming the House of Lords) and the Commons (House of Commons).

60 | Charlotte, Emily, and Anne.

61 | The three strategic-nuclear-weapons delivery systems are long-range bombers (air), land-based intercontinental ballistic missiles (land), and submarine-launched ballistic missiles (sea).

62 | Faith, hope, and charity.

63 | Minnesota Mining & Manufacturing (Company).

64 | Patti (or Patty), Maxene (or Maxine), and LaVerne.

65 | (Usually) swimming, bicycling, and distance running.

66 | The three stories in Gertrude Stein's 1909 collection are "The Good Anna," "Melanctha," and "The Gentle Lena."

67 | Heaven, Purgatory, and Hell. Prior to the Second Vatican Council, 1965, the souls of unbaptized infants and of the saints who lived before Christ were said to go to Limbo.

68 | John Ritter (Jack Tripper), Joyce DeWitt (Janet Wood), and Suzanne Somers (Chrissy Snow). After 1980, Somers was replaced by Jenilee Harrison (Cindy Snow) and then Priscilla Barnes (Terri Alden).

69 | Theology, law, and medicine.

70 | Al, Jim, and Harry. (Their real last name was Joachim.)

71 | First World: the major industrialized nations, including those in Western Europe, the United States, Canada, and Japan.

Second World: the USSR and the socialist countries of Eastern Europe.

Third World: politically nonaligned and economically underdeveloped countries, especially in Africa and Asia.

72 | The original members of this folk-singing group, popular in the late fifties and sixties, were Dave Guard, Nick Reynolds, and Bob Shane. John Stewart replaced Guard in 1961.

73 | A back who can run, pass, and punt.

74 | Solid, liquid, and gas. (Scientists also recognize a fourth state, plasma.)

75 | *Star Wars* (1977), *The Empire Strikes Back* (1980), and *Return of the Jedi* (1983).

76 | The Axis Powers Germany, Italy, and Japan signed the Tripartite Pact on September 27, 1940.

77 | Zsa Zsa (born Sari), Eva, and Magda.

78 | Dom, Joe, and Vince.

79 | Executive, legislative, and judicial.

80 | Tom Selleck, Ted Danson, and Steve Guttenberg.

81 | The butcher, the baker, the candlestick-maker.

82 | Shadrach, Meshach, and Abednego.

83 | Ann Sothern, Linda Darnell, and Jeanne Crain.

84 | The Battle of the Three Emperors at Austerlitz (December 2, 1805) pitted Napoleon I against Czar Alexander I (Russia) and Emperor Francis II (Austria). Napoleon won.

85 | The original Supremes were Diana Ross, Mary Wilson, and Florence Ballard. Cindy Birdsong replaced Florence Ballard in 1967.

86 | North America, Western Europe, and Japan.

87 | Robert Taylor, Franchot Tone, and Robert Young were the trio who loved Margaret Sullavan in the 1938 film *Three Comrades*.

88 | The first family consists of "up" and "down" quarks, the constituents of protons and neutrons; the electron; and a particle called the electron neutrino. The second family consists of "charmed" and "strange" quarks, muons, and muon neutrinos. The third is made up of "top" and "bottom" quarks, tau particles, and tau neutrinos.

89 | The three dramas by Aeschylus that make up the *Oresteia* (first performed in 458 B.C.) are *Agamemnon*, *The Libation Bearers* (*Choephoroi*), and the *Eumenides*.

90 | (Johann Sebastian) Bach, (Ludwig van) Beethoven, and (Johannes) Brahms.

91 | The three films in which Satyajit Ray told the story of Apu are *Pather Panchali* (1955), *Aparajito* (1956), and *The World of Apu* (1959).

92 | In this last of the late-sixteenth-century Wars of Religion in France, the contenders were King Henri III; Henri I de Lorraine, the duc de Guise; and Henri of Bourbon, king of Navarre (later Henri IV).

93 | The *Niña*, the *Pinta*, and the *Santa Maria*.

94 | The Nazi regime in Germany lasted from January 1933 to May 1945.

The Holy Roman Empire of 800 to 1806 was the First Reich, and the German Empire from 1871 to 1918 was the Second Reich.

4

95 | Pestilence, war, famine, and death, perched on, respectively, white, red, black, and pale horses.

96 | The Four Freedoms, as put forth by President Franklin D. Roosevelt on January 6, 1941, were freedom of speech, freedom of worship, freedom from want, and freedom from fear.

97 | Why is this night different from all other nights? (Overall question)

1. On all other nights we eat bread or matzoh. Why tonight do we eat only matzoh?
2. On all other nights we eat all kinds of herbs. Why tonight do we eat only bitter herbs?
3. On all other nights we eat herbs without dipping them into anything. Why tonight do we dip them twice into salt water?
4. On all other nights we eat either sitting up or reclining. Why tonight do we all recline?

98 | The four who were tried and imprisoned after the death of Mao Tse-tung (or Mao Zedong) for their activities during the Cultural Revolution were Chiang Ch'ing (or Jiang Qing), Mao's second wife; Wang Hung-wen (Wang Hongwen); Chang Ch'un-ch'iao (Zhang Chunqiao); and Yao Wen-yüan (Yao Wenyuan).

99 | Head, heart, hands, and health. The members pledge:

My Head to clearer thinking,
My Heart to greater loyalty,
My Hands to larger service, and
My Health to better living.

100 | In the 1975 sequel to the previous year's *The Three Musketeers* (actually made at the same time), the four were Oliver Reed (Athos), Frank Finlay (Porthos), Richard Chamberlain (Aramis), and Michael York (D'Artagnan).

101 | The four humours, or body liquids, are blood, phlegm, yellow bile, and black bile, corresponding to the four principal temperaments: sanguine, phlegmatic, choleric, and melancholic.

102 | *Justine* (1957), *Balthazar* (1958), *Mountolive* (1958), and *Clea* (1960).

103 | The Beatles: John Lennon, Paul McCartney, Ringo Starr, and George Harrison.

104 | The four truths as set forth by Buddha are:
1. Life is suffering.
2. The cause of suffering is craving, or desire.
3. Suffering can be ended through the extinction of desire.
4. The means to this is the Eightfold Path. (See *Eightfold Path*, page 129.)

105 | Colorado, New Mexico, Arizona, and Utah.

106 | In December 1978, two years after the death of Mao Zedong, the political leadership in China outlined four goals of modernization: of agriculture, industry, national defense, and science and technology.

107 | The four writers of the Gospels are Matthew, Mark, Luke, and John.

108 | Gravity, electromagnetism, the "strong" force, and the "weak" force.

109 | First International: The International Workingmen's Association, founded in London in 1864 to advance Socialist principles and unite the workers of all nations. One of its leaders was Karl Marx. It was dissolved in 1876.

Second International: Also called the Socialist International. An organization founded in Paris in 1889 to celebrate the hundredth anniversary of the French Revolution and to promote the unity of Socialist parties and trade unions in various countries. It was influential up to the outbreak of World War I.

Third International: Also called the Communist International (Comintern). An organization established in Moscow in 1919 under the leadership of the Bolsheviks and composed of Communist parties of various countries. Its aim was to promote world revolution. It was dissolved by Stalin in 1943.

Fourth International: A multinational association of Trotskyist organizations formed in 1938 in opposition to the Stalinist-dominated Third International. It had achieved little influence by the time of Trotsky's death in 1940.

110 | 1. Sunshine.
2. Rain.
3. The roses that bloom in the lane.
4. Somebody I adore.

111 | These four basic texts of Confucianism are the *Analects*, by Confucius himself (the Supreme Sage);

the *Mencius,* by Meng-tzu (the Second Sage); the *Great Learning;* and the *Doctrine of the Mean.*

112 | This long poem consists of four parts originally published at four different times: "Burnt Norton" (1936), "East Coker" (1940), "The Dry Salvages" (1941), and "Little Gidding" (1942).

113 | Chico, Harpo, Groucho, and Zeppo. After *Duck Soup* in 1933, Zeppo no longer appeared as one of the Marx Brothers.

114 | Boreas or Aquilo, the north wind; Zephyrus or Favonius, the west; Notus or Auster, the south; and Eurus, the east.

115 | This industrial complex consists of Rock Island, Moline, and East Moline, Illinois; and Davenport, Iowa.

116 | Ancient Greek and medieval philosophers believed that the four fundamental substances of which the universe was composed were earth, air, fire, and water.

117 | *Das Rheingold, Die Walküre, Siegfried,* and *Götterdämmerung* are the four operas of Wagner's *Ring* cycle, first performed together at Bayreuth in 1876.

118 | The milk group (milk and other dairy products); the meat group (meat, poultry, fish, eggs, legumes); the vegetable-fruit group; and the bread-cereals group (breads, cereals, pastas, flours).

119 | Soprano, tenor, alto, and bass.

120 | The four members of this group, best known for
a string of Motown hits in the sixties, are Levi
Stubbs (lead singer), Renaldo "Obie" Benson, Law-
rence Payton, and Abdul "Duke" Fakir.

121 | The four virtues as presented by Plato are wis-
dom (or prudence), courage (or fortitude), tem-
perance, and justice.

122 | The United States, Britain, France, and Japan
signed a treaty on December 13, 1921, pledging
that they would respect one another's rights in the Pacific Ocean and that all four would be consulted in the
event of a dispute between two of them over "any Pacific question."

123 | According to classical mythology, the decline of
humankind could be traced through Four Ages:
Golden, Silver, Bronze, and Iron. The Golden Age was
a time when human beings, newly created by the gods,
never labored, never warred, and never grew old. Per-
petual spring reigned. It was succeeded by the Silver
Age, in which the year was divided into seasons and
humans were forced to work. In the Bronze Age men
were violent and fought with one another. Finally came
the Iron Age, when evil prevailed: crime, war, and the
love of gain.

124 | Members of the press; the journalistic profes-
sion. The three other estates are the nobles, the
clergy, and the commons in pre-Revolution France; and
the Lords Temporal (barons and knights), Lords Spir-

itual (clergy), and the Commons in Great Britain. From a comment attributed to British statesman Edmund Burke by Thomas Carlyle: "Burke said there were Three Estates in Parliament; but, in the Reporters' Gallery yonder, there sat a Fourth Estate more important far than they all." But Carlyle may have been thinking of Lord Macaulay, who wrote in 1828: "The gallery in which the reporters sit has become a fourth estate of the realm."

125 | Sir Anthony Blunt. Blunt, Guy Burgess, Donald Maclean, and Harold "Kim" Philby were four members of the British establishment who became covert agents of the Soviet Union in the thirties and continued their activities into the fifties and sixties. Burgess and Maclean, both members of the Foreign Office, defected in 1951 and Philby, an intelligence officer, in 1964, but it wasn't until 1979 that Blunt, who had worked for MI5, the Security Service, was revealed as the "fourth man" in the spy network.

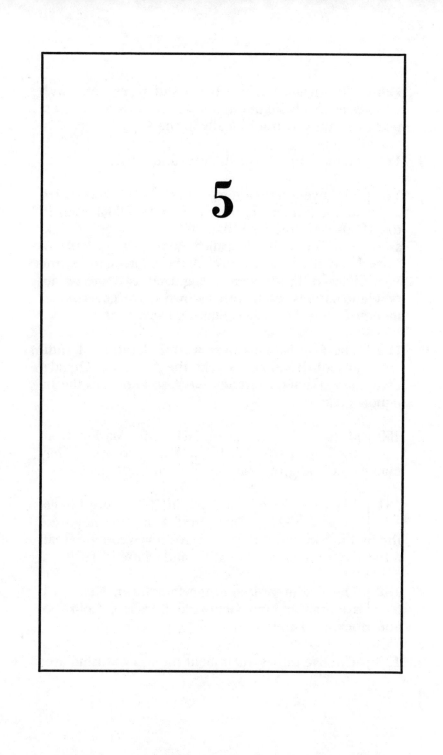

5

126 | Who, what, when, where, and why: along with *how*, the basic questions that a news story is expected to answer, traditionally in the lead.

127 | Sight, hearing, smell, taste, and touch.

128 | The five Southeastern tribes who were resettled in the Indian Territory (eastern Oklahoma) in the 1830s were the Cherokee, Creek, Choctaw, Chickasaw, and Seminole. So called because they had absorbed much of the culture of the white settlers, the Five Civilized Tribes were recognized as domestic dependent nations, each with its own tribal government modeled after the United States government.

129 | The Five Nations were a confederation of Indians of Iroquoian stock: the Mohawk, Oneida, Onondaga, Cayuga, and Seneca. Also known as the Iroquois League.

130 | Michael, Tito, Jermaine, Jackie, and Marlon, from 1968 to 1975. In 1976, Randy replaced Jermaine, and the group became known as the Jacksons.

131 | The celebrity quints, born in 1934, were Émilie, Yvonne, Cécile, Marie, and Annette. They were the first known quintuplets to have survived more than a few days. Émilie died in 1954 and Marie in 1970.

132 | The five organized-crime families in New York are the Gambino, Genovese, Lucchese, Colombo, and Bonanno families.

133 | The five duties incumbent on every Muslim are:

1. *Shahāda,* or profession of the faith ("There is no god but Allah," and "Muhammad is the prophet of Allah").
2. *Salāt,* or ritual prayer.
3. *Zakāt,* or obligatory almsgiving.
4. *Sawm,* or fasting during the month of Ramadān from dawn until sunset.
5. *Hajj,* or the pilgrimage to Mecca, which must be made at least once in a lifetime.

134 | Manhattan, the Bronx, Brooklyn, Queens, and Staten Island.

135 | The five stages of dying—and by extension any grievous loss—as outlined by Elisabeth Kübler-Ross are:

1. Denial. ("No, not me.")
2. Rage and anger. ("Why me?")
3. Bargaining. ("Maybe if I ask nicely, or maybe if I do this . . .")
4. Depression.
5. Acceptance. ("Yes, me.")

136 | The first five books of the Old Testament, also called the Law of Moses, are Genesis, Exodus, Leviticus, Numbers, and Deuteronomy.

137 | Stoke-on-Trent, Burslem, Hanley, Longton, Tunstall (the "Five Towns" that provide the setting for Arnold Bennett's best-known novels), and Fenton constitute this district in Staffordshire, England. Also called The Potteries, it is noted for its production of china and earthenware.

138 | First position: The feet are turned outward in a straight line, with the heels touching each other.

Second position: The feet are turned outward in a straight line, about twelve inches apart, with the weight equally divided between them.

Third position: The feet are turned out and placed one in front of the other so that the heel of the front foot fits into the hollow of the instep of the back foot.

Fourth position: Both feet are turned out, one in front of the other about twelve inches apart, with the weight evenly distributed.

Fifth position: Both feet are turned out and touching each other, placed so that the big toe of the back foot protrudes just beyond the heel of the front foot.

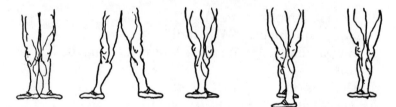

Illustrations copyright © 1990 Edward Bennett.

139 | This group of late-nineteenth-century Russian composers, united by their efforts to write music of a distinctively Russian character, were Mily Balakirev, César Cui, Aleksandr Borodin, Modest Mussorgsky, and Nikolay Rimsky-Korsakov.

140 | Atlantic, Pacific, Indian, Arctic, and Antarctic.

141 | Lakes Erie, Huron, Michigan, Ontario, and Superior.

142 | The *Wu Ching* (Five Classics), central in Chinese education for two thousand years, are the *I Ching,* or *Book of Changes;* the *Shu Ching,* or *Book of History;* the *Shih Ching,* or *Book of Poetry* (or *Odes*); the *Li Chi,* or *Book of Rites;* and the *Ch'un Ch'iu,* or *Spring and Autumn Annals.*

143 | First Republic: the republic proclaimed in 1792 as a result of the French Revolution; replaced by the First Empire (under Napoleon I) in 1804.

Second Republic: the republic established in 1848 under Louis-Napoléon and succeeded by the Second Empire in 1852.

Third Republic: the government that lasted from the fall of Louis-Napoléon in 1870 until the German occupation in 1940.

Fourth Republic: the republic established in 1946 and succeeded by the Fifth Republic in 1958.

Fifth Republic: the republic established in 1958 under Charles de Gaulle.

144 | Styx (river of hate); Acheron (river of grief, or woe); Phlegethon (river of liquid fire); Cocytus (river of wailing, or lamentation); and Lethe (river of forgetfulness, or oblivion).

145 | In ancient Greece the pentathlon consisted of a footrace, long jump, javelin throw, discus throw, and wrestling. In the modern Olympics it consists of fencing, horseback riding, pistol shooting, cross-country running, and swimming.

146 | The title characters of the children's classic *Five Little Peppers and How They Grew* (first published in 1881) and its eleven sequels were Ben, Polly, Joel, Davie, and Phronsie. The author, Harriet Stone, wrote under the name Margaret Sidney.

147 | In ancient Chinese philosophy, the five elements (*Wu hsing*) or fundamental forces of the universe are wood, fire, earth, metal, and water, which succeed and interact with one another and which govern the seasons, the cycles of history, the planets, numbers, colors, and many other phenomena.

148 | In the 1960 *Five Branded Women*, a film directed by Martin Ritt, Jeanne Moreau, Vera Miles, Silvana Mangano, Barbara Bel Geddes, and Carla Gravina play five Yugoslavians who, despised by the partisans for having consorted with a Nazi officer, ultimately prove they have the right stuff.

149 | A group of subversive agents within a country who collaborate with the enemy. The term was originally applied to Franco sympathizers during the Spanish Civil War by a fascist revolutionary general who, as four of his army columns moved on Madrid, referred to his supporters there as his "fifth column."

150 | According to the Pythagoreans, the fifth essence (quintessence) is ether, of which the heavenly bodies are composed and which is latent in all things. The other four are earth, air, fire, and water.

151 | A sect of Puritans who, during the Commonwealth in England in the seventeenth century, believed the fifth monarchy—the reign of Christ—was at hand and they should help bring it about by force. The first four monarchies were the Assyrian, Persian, Greek, and Roman.

6

152 | First Day: light.

Second day: the firmament (Heaven) separating the waters above from the waters below.

Third day: dry land (Earth) and vegetation.

Fourth day: the sun, the moon, and the stars.

Fifth day: the creatures of the sea and of the air (birds).

Sixth day: the creatures of the earth (animals); and man (humans).

(On the seventh day He rested.)

153 | The six flags from which the Six Flags amusement parks take their name are those that, at one time or another, flew over Texas: Spain, from 1519 to 1685 and 1690 to 1821; France, from 1685 to 1690; Mexico, from 1821 to 1836; Republic of Texas, from 1836 to 1845; the Confederacy, from 1861 to 1865; and the United States, from 1845 to 1861 and 1865 to the present.

154 | Catherine of Aragon (mother of future queen Mary I), Anne Boleyn (mother of future queen Elizabeth I), Jane Seymour (mother of Henry's successor, Edward VI), Anne of Cleves, Catherine Howard, and Catherine Parr.

155 | This confederation of Iroquois tribes consisted of the Five Nations—the Mohawk, Oneida, Onondaga, Cayuga, and Seneca—plus, after 1722, the Tuscarora.

156 | The members of this informal group of French twentieth-century composers, whose music represented a revolt against the Romanticism of Wagner and the Impressionism of Debussy, were Francis Poulenc, Darius Milhaud, Arthur Honegger, Georges Auric, Louis Durey, and Germaine Tailleferre.

157 The six virtues or perfections (*pāramitās*) practiced by a bodhisattva, or aspiring buddha, on the path of enlightenment are (1) generosity, or charity; (2) moral conduct; (3) patience, or forbearance; (4) vigor; (5) concentration (meditation); and (6) wisdom.

158 According to Aristotle, the six elements of tragedy, as defined in his *Poetics,* are plot; character; thought; diction, or language; melody; and spectacle.

159 The six characters seeking a dramatic framework in Luigi Pirandello's *Six Characters in Search of an Author* (1921) are The Father, The Mother, The Stepdaughter, The Son, The Boy, and The Child.

160 The six counties of the former Irish province of Ulster are Antrim, Armagh, Down, Fermanagh, Londonderry (also called Derry), and Tyrone.

161 The films that make up director Eric Rohmer's cycle of *six contes moraux* are *La Boulangère de Monceau* (1962), a short; *La Carrière de Suzanne* (1963), a sixty-minute featurette; *La Collectionneuse* (1967); *My Night at Maud's* (*Ma Nuit chez Maud,* 1969); *Claire's Knee* (*Le Genou de Claire,* 1970); and *Chloe in the Afternoon* (*L'amour l'après-midi,* 1972).

162 In *Six Crises,* a memoir published in 1962, Richard Nixon discussed six significant episodes in his political career:

1. *The Hiss Case.* Nixon played a crucial role in the investigation that led to the indictment of Alger Hiss, who in 1950 was convicted of perjury regarding his involvement with Whittaker Chambers, a former courier for the Communist party. The case brought Nixon national attention.
2. *The 1952 Fund Speech.* While running for vice president in 1952, Nixon, then a senator, was accused of receiving a supplementary salary of twenty thousand dollars per year contributed by a group of California businessmen. He responded to the charges in the famous "Checkers" television speech, in which he admitted having accepted the gift of a cocker spaniel.
3. *President Eisenhower's Heart Attack.* In 1955 Nixon, as vice president, found himself briefly on the threshold of the presidency when Eisenhower suffered a (nonfatal) heart attack.
4. *Caracas.* On a trip to South America in 1958, Vice President Nixon was the target of anti-American demonstrators, especially in Caracas, where hostile crowds spat on him and hurled rocks at his car.
5. *The "Kitchen Debate" with Khrushchev.* In 1959, Nixon had a highly publicized confrontation with Soviet leader Nikita Khrushchev in a model American kitchen at a Moscow exhibit.
6. *The Campaign of 1960.* In a hard-fought campaign for the presidency, Nixon was narrowly defeated by John F. Kennedy.

163 | The Lord said to Joshua: "Speak to the children of Israel, saying, Appoint out for you cities of refuge . . . that the slayer that killeth any person unawares and unwittingly may flee thither: and they shall be your refuge from the avenger of blood." (Joshua

20:2–3.) The six cities were Kedesh; Shechem; Kirjath-arba, which is Hebron; Bezer; Ramoth; and Golan.

164 | Extrasensory perception (beyond sight, smell, hearing, taste, and touch).

7

165 | The immortal septet in Disney's *Snow White and the Seven Dwarfs* (1937) are Dopey, Sleepy, Doc, Grumpy, Happy, Sneezy, and Bashful.

166 | Pride, avarice (or covetousness or greed), anger, envy, lust, gluttony, and sloth.

167 | The Pyramids of Giza in Egypt; the Hanging Gardens of Babylon; the Statue of Zeus at Olympia; the Temple of Artemis at Ephesus; the Mausoleum of Halicarnassus; the Colossus of Rhodes; the Pharos (Lighthouse) of Alexandria.

168 | At first the infant,
Mewling and puking in the nurse's arms.
And then the whining schoolboy, with his satchel
And shining morning face, creeping like snail
Unwillingly to school. And then the lover,
Sighing like furnace, with a woful ballad
Made to his mistress' eyebrow. Then a soldier,
Full of strange oaths, and bearded like the pard,
Jealous in honor, sudden and quick in quarrel,
Seeking the bubble reputation
Even in the cannon's mouth. And then the justice,
In fair round belly with good capon lin'd,
With eyes severe and beard of formal cut,
Full of wise saws and modern instances;
And so he plays his part. The sixth age shifts
Into the lean and slipper'd pantaloon,
With spectacles on nose and pouch on side,
His youthful hose, well sav'd, a world too wide
For his shrunk shank; and his big manly voice,
Turning again toward childish treble, pipes
And whistles in his sound. Last scene of all,
That ends this strange eventful history,
Is second childishness, and mere oblivion,
Sans teeth, sans eyes, sans taste, sans everything.

—As You Like It

169 | The seven hills on which ancient Rome was built are the Aventine, Caelian, Capitoline, Esquiline, Palatine, Quirinal, and Viminal.

170 | The seven mythical heroes who led an expedition against Thebes, the subject of a tragedy by Aeschylus, were Adrastus, Amphiaraus, Capaneus, Hippomedon, Parthenopaeus, Polynices, and Tydeus. (Some accounts substitute Mecisteus and Eteoclus for Polynices and Tydeus.)

171 | Rennie Davis, David Dellinger, John Froines, Tom Hayden, Abbie Hoffman, Jerry Rubin, and Lee Weiner were the seven antiwar activists put on trial for their role in the disturbances outside the Democratic National Convention in Chicago in 1968. Bobby Seale, one of the original eight defendants, was tried separately.

172 | In Greek mythology, the seven daughters of Atlas and the nymph Pleione (known as the Seven Sisters) are Alcyone, Celaeno, Electra, Maia, Merope, Sterope (or Asterope), and Taygete. They were transformed into stars of the same name. The "lost Pleiad," or faintest star of the constellation, is either Merope, concealing herself out of shame for having loved a mortal, or Electra, who is grieving for Troy, her son's city.

173 | Pierre de Ronsard, Joachim du Bellay, Jean-Antoine de Baïf, Étienne Jodelle, Pontus de Tyard, Rémy Belleau, and Jean Dorat were the French Renaissance poets, collectively known as La Pléiade, who attempted to revitalize French literature by using classical works as their models and inspiration.

174 | Yul Brynner (Chris), Steve McQueen (Vin), Horst
Buchholz (Chico), Charles Bronson (O'Reilly),
Robert Vaughn (Lee), James Coburn (Britt), and Brad
Dexter (Harry) were the Americans who rode into town
in *The Magnificent Seven* (1960). Eli Wallach played Cal-
vero, the Mexican bandit leader.

175 | The seven rites that confer grace are baptism,
confirmation, the Eucharist (Communion),
penance, holy orders (the priesthood), matrimony, and
anointing of the sick (extreme unction, or last rites).

176 | The original Seven Sister colleges were Barnard,
Bryn Mawr, Mount Holyoke, Radcliffe, Smith,
Vassar, and Wellesley. Vassar is now coed; Radcliffe
has merged with Harvard College.

177 | The battles in which the Confederate Army drove
back the Union Army in its attempt to capture
Richmond in 1862 were: Battle of Oak Grove (June
25); Mechanicsville (June 26); Gaines's Mill (June 27);
Savage's Station (June 29); Frayser's Farm (June 30);
and Malvern Hill (July 1). For the Union troops most
of June 28 was spent marching toward their base at
Harrison's Landing.

178 | The seven main energy centers, or chakras, of
the body are:

1. The crown, or top of the head (*sahasrara*).
2. Between the eyebrows (*ajna*).
3. The throat (*vishuddha* or *visuddha*).
4. The heart (*anahata*).
5. The solar plexus region (*manipura*).
6. The lower abdominal area (*svadhisthana*).
7. The root, or base of the spine (*muladhara*).

179 | Mechanical, chemical, heat, atomic, light, electrical, and solar.

180 | The four cardinal (or natural or Platonic) virtues—wisdom, courage, temperance, and justice —and the three Christian theological virtues—faith, hope, and charity.

181 | In *The Arabian Nights* (or *The Thousand and One Nights*) Sindbad the Sailor tells the story of the following seven voyages:

1. On his way to India Sindbad's ship is becalmed, and he and some of his crew decide to visit a small nearby island. But the "island" turns out to be a sleeping whale, and when the whale wakes up, Sindbad and the others are cast into the sea. Eventually Sindbad manages to return to his ship and sails home.

2. Sindbad is left behind on a deserted island, where he discovers a huge roc's egg. When the roc returns to the nest, Sindbad ties himself to the bird's leg. The roc flies to a valley strewn with large diamonds. Sindbad has heard that merchants throw great hunks of fresh meat into the valley to which the diamonds stick; when the eagles pick up the meat and return to their nests, the merchants frighten them away and recover the diamonds. Sindbad fastens himself to a hunk of meat and is carried away by an eagle to its nest. With the help of a group of merchants, he finally returns home.

3. Sindbad is shipwrecked on an island where he encounters savage dwarfs and a monstrous one-eyed giant. He and his fellow sailors blind the giant, but two other ogres help the blind one give chase, and only Sindbad escapes to safety.

4. Again Sindbad is shipwrecked, this time on an island inhabited by cannibals. He escapes and meets a group of men who take him to their kingdom, where he marries a high-born lady. When she dies, he is buried alive with her according to the custom of the country. He follows an animal out of the tomb and hails a ship home.

5. Angry rocs hurl stones on Sindbad's ship and wreck it. On an island on which he takes refuge, he comes across the Old Man of the Sea and offers to carry him on his back. But the old man refuses to release his grip, and only by getting him drunk does Sindbad manage to escape.

6. Sindbad's ship is driven ashore on an uninhabited island. Sindbad builds a raft, which he rides on an underground river to the city of Serendib, situated in a valley formed by the highest mountain in the world. He visits the top of the mountain, a place filled with rare gems and exotic plants, where Adam was banished after being expelled from Paradise. After a long stay in Serendib, Sindbad sails home.

7. Pirates seize Sindbad's ship and sell him into slavery. His master, an ivory merchant, orders him to shoot an elephant a day. One day an elephant picks Sindbad up and transports him to an elephant burial ground, which is covered with ivory tusks. His master, delighted with the discovery, grants Sindbad his freedom, and Sindbad returns home laden with riches.

182 | The seven churches in Asia Minor referred to by John in the Book of Revelation are located in Ephesus, Smyrna, Pergamos (Pergamum), Thyatira, Sardis, Philadelphia, and Laodicea.

183 | The brothers: Howard Keel (Adam); Marc Platt (Daniel); Jeff Richards (Benjamin); Matt Mattox (Caleb); Russ Tamblyn (Gideon); Tommy Rall (Frank); and Jacques d'Amboise (Ephraim).

The brides: Jane Powell (Milly); Virginia Gibson (Liza); Julie Newmeyer, later Newmar (Dorcas); Nancy Kilges (Alice); Ruta Kilmonis, later Lee (Ruth); Betty Carr (Sarah); and Norma Doggett (Martha).

184 | According to Christian and Islamic legend, seven Christian youths, persecuted by the Roman emperor Decius, took refuge in a cave near Ephesus in A.D. 250. The emperor walled up the cave, and the seven fell into a sleep that lasted some two hundred years. When the cave was reopened, the sleepers awoke. Their names were Constantine, Dionysius, John, Maximian, Malchus, Martinian, and Serapion.

185 | Corfu, Cephalonia, Ithaca, Leukas, Paxos, and Zante (ancient name Zacynthus) off the west coast of Greece, and Cerigo (Cythera) off the south coast.

186 | The last words spoken by Jesus Christ on the cross were:

1. "Father, forgive them; for they know not what they do."
2. "Verily I say unto thee, Today shalt thou be with me in paradise."
3. "Woman, behold thy son! . . . Behold thy mother!"
4. "Eli [Eloi], Eli [Eloi], lama sabachthani? . . . My God, my God, why hast thou forsaken me?"
5. "I thirst."
6. "It is finished."
7. "Father, into thy hands I commend my spirit."

187 | The seven major industrialized nations, whose representatives meet every year to discuss economic issues, are the United States, Canada, Great Britain, France, Italy, West Germany, and Japan.

188 | The seven national patron saints, subject of a medieval romance by Richard Johnson, are Saint George of England; Saint Denis, or Denys, of France; Saint James of Spain; Saint Anthony of Italy; Saint Andrew of Scotland; Saint Patrick of Ireland; and Saint David of Wales.

189 | The seven branches of learning during the Middle Ages were grammar, logic, and rhetoric (the trivium); and arithmetic, music, geometry, and astronomy (the quadrivium).

190 | The Baby Bells, the seven major providers of local telephone service, are:

NYNEX, which serves New York and New England.

Pacific Telesis, which serves California and Nevada.

U.S. West, based in Denver and serving an area from Washington State east to Minnesota and south to New Mexico and Arizona.

BellSouth, based in Atlanta and serving much of the South.

Southwestern Bell Corporation, based in St. Louis and serving the South from Arkansas through Texas and into Missouri.

Ameritech (American Information Technologies), which serves the Great Lakes region.

Bell Atlantic, based in Philadelphia and serving much of the Eastern seaboard.

191 | The most commonly mentioned "seven wise men," politicians and philosophers of ancient Greece, were Bias, Chilon, Cleobulus, Periander, Pittacus, Solon, and Thales.

192 | The seven sorrows, or dolors, of the Blessed Virgin are:

1. The prophecy of Simeon.
2. The flight into Egypt.
3. The three-day separation from Jesus in Jerusalem.
4. Meeting Jesus on the way to Calvary.
5. The Crucifixion.
6. The removal of Christ's body from the cross.
7. The burial in the tomb.

193 | The seven joys of the Blessed Virgin are:

1. Annunciation.
2. Visitation.
3. Nativity.
4. Epiphany (Adoration of the Magi).
5. Finding Jesus in the Temple.
6. Resurrection.
7. Assumption.

194 | William Empson, in an influential critical work of that title first published in 1930, discussed seven types of ambiguity, which he defined as "any verbal nuance . . . which gives room for alternative reactions to the same piece of language."

1. The first type of ambiguity occurs when "a word or a grammatical structure is effective in several ways at once," through metaphor and other devices.
2. In the second type, "two or more alternative meanings are fully resolved into one," as in the lines "But change she earth, or change she sky, / Yet I will love her till I die": "*Change* may mean 'move to another' or 'alter the one you have got,' and *earth* may be the lady's private world, or the poet's, or that of mankind at large."
3. Two apparently unconnected meanings are given simultaneously, as in a pun, or, by extension, in allegory and pastoral, when there is reference to more than one "universe of discourse."
4. Here the alternative meanings "combine to make clear a complicated state of mind in the author."
5. The fifth type occurs "when the author is discovering his idea in the act of writing, or not holding it all in his mind at once."
6. In the sixth type, what is said is meaningless or contradictory, so that the reader is forced to invent interpretations.
7. The seventh type is the most ambiguous, "when the two meanings of the word . . . are the two opposite meanings defined by the context, so that the effect is to show a fundamental division in the author's mind."

195 | In Japanese folklore, the seven gods of happiness and good fortune, the Shichi-fuku-jin, are Bishamon, patron of warriors; Daikoku, god of wealth and guardian of farmers; Ebisu, patron of tradesmen and fishermen; Fukurokuju, god of wisdom and longevity; Hotei, god of good humor; Jurojin, also god of longevity; and Benten, goddess of feminine beauty, music, and the arts.

196 | The seven actresses who appeared in John Ford's 1966 film are Anne Bancroft, Margaret Leighton, Sue Lyon, Mildred Dunnock, Flora Robson, Betty Field, and Anna Lee.

197 | The seven gifts of the Holy Ghost, said to be infused into the soul at baptism, are wisdom, understanding, counsel, fortitude, knowledge, piety, and fear of the Lord.

198 | According to the Mohammedan and cabalist systems, there are seven levels of heaven, each rising above the other. The seventh is the highest level; thus the term *seventh heaven* has become synonymous with ultimate bliss.

199 | The eight Chicago White Sox players who were brought up on charges of having accepted money to throw the 1919 World Series were Joe Jackson, Eddie Cicotte, Lefty Williams, Chick Gandil, Fred McMullin, Happy Felsch, Buck Weaver, and Swede Risberg. Known thereafter as the "Black Sox," they were the subject of a novel by Eliot Asinof and a 1988 movie based on the novel, both called *Eight Men Out*.

200 | John Sayles's 1988 movie, *Eight Men Out*, starred D. B. Sweeney as "Shoeless" Joe Jackson, John Cusack as Buck Weaver, David Strathairn as Eddie Cicotte, Charlie Sheen as Hap Felsch, Michael Rooker as Chick Gandil, Perry Lang as Fred McMullin, James Read as Lefty Williams, and Don Harvey as Swede Risberg.

201 | The Eightfold Path is the fourth of Buddha's Four Noble Truths: (1) existence is suffering; (2) suffering is caused by desire; (3) desire can be overcome by (4) following the Eightfold Path:

1. Right understanding or belief.
2. Right thought or purpose.
3. Right speech.
4. Right action or conduct.
5. Right means of livelihood.
6. Right effort.
7. Right mindfulness.
8. Right concentration or meditation.

202 | In Clement Clarke Moore's "A Visit from St. Nicholas" (" 'Twas the night before Christmas . . ."), written in 1822, the reindeer are called Dasher, Dancer, Prancer, Vixen, Comet, Cupid, Donder, and Blitzen.

203 | This group of American Realist painters, who held a group exhibition in 1908, consisted of Robert Henri, Maurice Prendergast, John Sloan, George Luks, Everett Shinn, William J. Glackens, Ernest Lawson, and Arthur B. Davies. Later, with five others, they became known as the Ashcan School.

204 | The eight blessings pronounced by Jesus in the Sermon on the Mount are:

1. Blessed are the poor in spirit: for theirs is the kingdom of heaven.
2. Blessed are they that mourn: for they shall be comforted.
3. Blessed are the meek: for they shall inherit the earth.
4. Blessed are they which do hunger and thirst after righteousness: for they shall be filled.
5. Blessed are the merciful: for they shall obtain mercy.
6. Blessed are the pure in heart: for they shall see God.
7. Blessed are the peacemakers: for they shall be called the children of God.
8. Blessed are they which are persecuted for righteousness' sake: for theirs is the kingdom of heaven.

Sometimes a ninth Beatitude is included: Blessed are ye, when men shall revile you, and persecute you, and shall say all manner of evil against you falsely, for my sake.

205 | The popular brood in the television show of the late seventies and early eighties:

The Children: Nicholas (Adam Rich); Tommy (Willie Aames); Elizabeth (Connie Needham); Nancy (Dianne Kay); Susan (Susan Richardson); Joannie (Laurie Walters); Mary (Lani O'Grady); and David (Grant Goodeve).

The Adults: Tom Bradford, the father (Dick Van Patten); Joan Bradford, the mother (Diana Hyland, who died after four episodes); and Abby Bradford, new wife (Betty Buckley).

206 | The eight colleges of the Big Eight athletic conference: University of Colorado, Iowa State, University of Kansas, Kansas State University, University of Missouri, University of Nebraska, University of Oklahoma, and Oklahoma State University.

207 | The Eight Trigrams (Pa Kua) are all the possible combinations of broken and unbroken lines, arranged in eight sets of threes, which form the basis of ancient Chinese divination and philosophy, notably the *I Ching*. They are: *k'an*, represented by the moon and moving water (rain or streams); *ch'ien*, heaven; *k'un*, earth; *li*, fire, sun, lightning; *chên*, thunder; *sun*, wind; *kên*, mountain; and *tui*, collected water (lake).

208 | V8 is made up of the juices of tomatoes, carrots, celery, beets, parsley, lettuce, watercress, and spinach.

209 | The Eight Immortals (Pa Hsien) are eight characters of Taoist mythology, mortals who followed the Tao (the way) and thus attained the status of immortality: Chung-li Ch'üan, Lü Tung-pin, Li T'ieh-kuai, Lan Ts'ai-ho, Chang Kuo-lao, Han Hsiang-tzu, Ts'ao Kuo-chiu, and Ho Hsien-ku.

9

210 | The nine daughters of Zeus and Mnemosyne who presided over various arts and sciences were: Calliope (epic poetry), Clio (history), Erato (love poetry), Euterpe (music), Melpomene (tragedy), Polyhymnia (sacred poetry and hymns), Terpsichore (dance), Thalia (comedy), and Urania (astronomy).

211 | The nine planets, in order nearest the sun, are Mercury, Venus, Earth, Mars, Jupiter, Saturn, Uranus, Neptune, and Pluto.

212 | These three sets of heroes, often grouped together in the Middle Ages, were Hector of Troy, Alexander the Great, and Julius Caesar (three pagans); Joshua, David, and Judas Maccabaeus (three Jews); and King Arthur, Charlemagne, and Godfrey of Bouillon, or Godefroi de Bouillon (three Christians).

213 | The nine orders of the celestial hierarchy are:

1. Seraphim, Cherubim, and Thrones in the first circle.
2. Dominions (or Dominations), Powers, and Virtues in the second circle.
3. Principalities (or Princedoms), Archangels, and Angels in the third circle.

214 | The nine books that comprise the Four Books and the Five Classics of the Confucian canon are the *Analects*, the *Mencius*, the *Great Learning*, and the *Doctrine of the Mean*; and the *I Ching* (*Book of Changes*), the *Shu Ching* (*Book of History*), the *Shih Ching* (*Book of Poetry*, or *Odes*), the *Li Chi* (*Book of Rites*), and the *Ch'un Ch'iu* (*Spring and Autumn Annals*).

215 | Great Britain, the United States, France, Japan, Italy, Belgium, the Netherlands, Portugal, and

China were the nine countries that signed a treaty at the Washington Conference on February 6, 1922, agreeing to respect China's territorial integrity, political independence, and neutrality in time of war, and to honor the right of all nations to do business with it on equal terms.

216 | *First Circle* (Limbo): The Virtuous Pagans (those who led blameless lives, but lived before the coming of Christ, hence were not baptized).

Second Circle (the beginning of Hell proper): The Lustful, or Carnal (those who sacrificed reason to passion).

Third Circle: The Gluttonous.

Fourth Circle: The Avaricious (misers) and the Prodigal (spendthrifts).

Fifth Circle: The Wrathful and the Sullen.

Sixth Circle: The Heretics.

Seventh Circle: This circle, housing the Violent, has three rings. In the first are confined the Violent Against Others; in the second, the Violent Against Self (suicides); in the third, the Violent Against God, Nature, and Art (blasphemers, sodomites, and usurers, respectively).

Eighth Circle (Malebolge): Malebolge is a funnel-shaped region made of gray stone surrounding a deep well. Divided into ten concentric trenches or chasms called bolgias, it contains the Fraudulent.
    In the First Bolgia: Panderers and Seducers.
    Second: Flatterers.
    Third: Simonists (those who traded the favor of the Church for money).

Fourth: Foretellers of the Future.
Fifth: Bribe Takers.
Sixth: Hypocrites.
Seventh: Thieves.
Eighth: Evil Counselors.
Ninth: Sowers of Discord/Scandal-mongers/Schismatics.
Tenth: Falsifiers (alchemists, impersonators, counterfeiters, false witnesses).

Ninth Circle (Cocytus): This is the frozen pit of Hell, the place where Traitors are confined. In the first rung are those who betrayed kin; in the second, betrayers of country; in the third, betrayers of their guests; in the fourth, betrayers of their masters (i.e., Judas Iscariot, Brutus, and Cassius).

217 | The nine anti–Vietnam War protesters who burned draft records in Catonsville, Maryland, in 1968 were Daniel Berrigan, the Reverend Philip Berrigan, David Darst, John Hogan, Thomas Lewis, Marjorie Melville, Thomas Melville, George Mische, and Mary Moylan. Later Daniel Berrigan wrote a dramatization of their trial, *The Trial of the Catonsville Nine.*

218 | The nine divisions of the universe in Norse mythology are Asgard, home of the Aesir gods; Vanaheim, home of the Vanir gods; Midgard, home of humankind; Alfheim, home of the light elves; Svartalfheim or Svartalfaheim, home of the dark elves; Jotünheim, home of the giants; Niflheim, land of darkness, cold, and eternal silence; Muspelheim or Muspellheim, land of fire and sun; and either Hel, realm of the dead, or Nidavellir, land of the dwarfs.

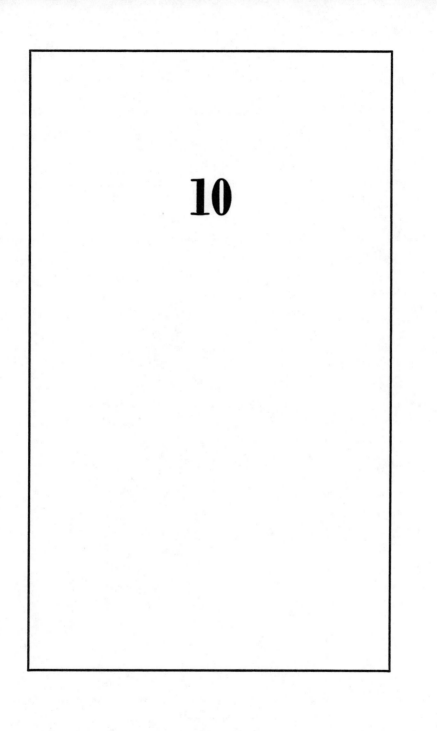

10

219 | 1. I am the Lord thy God, which have brought thee out of the land of Egypt, out of the house of bondage. Thou shalt have no other gods before me.

2. Thou shalt not make unto thee any graven image, or any likeness of any thing that is in heaven above, or that is in the earth beneath, or that is in the water underneath the earth: thou shalt not bow down thyself to them, nor serve them: for I the Lord thy God am a jealous God, visiting the iniquity of the fathers upon the children unto the third and fourth generation of them that hate me; and shewing mercy unto thousands of them that love me, and keep my commandments.

3. Thou shalt not take the name of the Lord thy God in vain; for the Lord will not hold him guiltless that taketh his name in vain.

4. Remember the sabbath day, to keep it holy. Six days shalt thou labour, and do all thy work: but the seventh day is the sabbath of the Lord thy God: in it thou shalt not do any work, thou, nor thy son, nor thy daughter, thy manservant, nor thy maidservant, nor thy cattle, nor thy stranger that is within thy gates: for in six days the Lord made heaven and earth, the sea, and all that in them is, and rested the seventh day: wherefore the Lord blessed the sabbath day, and hallowed it.

5. Honour thy father and thy mother: that thy days may be long upon the land which the Lord thy God giveth thee.

6. Thou shalt not kill.

7. Thou shalt not commit adultery.

8. Thou shalt not steal.
9. Thou shalt not bear false witness against thy neighbour.
10. Thou shalt not covet thy neighbour's house, thou shalt not covet thy neighbour's wife, nor his manservant, nor his maidservant, nor his ox, nor his ass, nor any thing that is thy neighbour's.

The above according to the King James Version of the Bible. In Roman Catholic and Lutheran tradition, the prohibitions against coveting another's wife and coveting his possessions are two separate commandments; the first two injunctions are regarded as one.

220 | The original nursery rhyme, as composed by Septimus Winner, goes:

Ten little Injuns standin' in a line,
One toddled home and then there were nine;
Nine little Injuns swingin' on a gate,
One tumbled off and then there were eight.

One little, two little, three little, four little, five little In-
jun boys.
Six little, seven little, eight little, nine little, ten little
Injun boys.

Eight little Injuns gayest under heav'n,
One went to sleep and then there were seven;
Seven little Injuns cutting up their tricks,
One broke his neck and then there were six.

Six little Injuns kickin' all alive,
One kick'd the bucket and then there were five;
Five little Injuns on a cellar door,
One tumbled in and then there were four.

Four little Injuns up on a spree,
One he got fuddled and then there were three;

Three little Injuns out in a canoe,
One tumbled overboard and then there were two.

Two little Injuns foolin' with a gun,
One shot t'other and then there was one;
One little Injun livin' all alone,
He got married and then there were none.

221 | Agatha Christie's murder mystery *Ten Little In-
dians,* previously published as *Ten Little Niggers*
and later retitled *And Then There Were None,* based its
structure on the 1869 song "Ten Little Niggers" by
Frank Green:

Ten little Indian boys went out to dine;
One choked his little self and then there were nine.

Nine little Indian boys sat up very late;
One overslept himself and then there were eight.

Eight little Indian boys traveling in Devon;
One said he'd stay and then there were seven.

Seven little Indian boys chopping up sticks;
One chopped himself in halves and then there
    were six.

Six little Indian boys playing with a hive;
A bumblebee stung one and then there were five.

Five little Indian boys going in for law;
One got in Chancery and then there were four.

Four little Indian boys going out to sea;
A red herring swallowed one and then there were three.

Three little Indian boys walking in the zoo;
A big bear hugged one and then there were two.

Two little Indian boys sitting in the sun;
One got frizzled up and then there was one.

One little Indian boy left all alone;
He went and hanged himself and then there were none.

The characters were:

1. Anthony Marston (one choked his little self).
2. Mrs. Rogers (one overslept himself).
3. General Macarthur (one said he'd stay there).
4. Mr. Rogers (one chopped himself).
5. Emily Brent (a bumblebee stung one).
6. Mr. Justice Wargrave (one got in Chancery).
7. Dr. Armstrong (a red herring swallowed one).
8. Mr. Blore (a big bear hugged one).
9. Captain Philip Lombard (one got frizzled up).
10. Vera Claythorne (he went and hanged himself).

222 | In this film adaptation of Agatha Christie's 1939 novel, the ten guilty parties were played by Hugh O'Brian, Shirley Eaton, Leo Genn, Wilfrid Hyde-White, Stanley Holloway, Fabian, Daliah Lavi, Dennis Price, Marianne Hoppe, and Mario Adorf.

223 | To convince the Pharaoh to release the Israelites from bondage, the Lord through Moses brought ten plagues upon Egypt:

1. All of the waters turned to blood.
2. Plague of frogs.
3. Plague of lice.
4. Plague of flies.
5. Plague of murrain (livestock disease).
6. Plague of boils on man and beast.
7. Plague of hail.
8. Plague of locusts.
9. Plague of darkness.
10. All first-born Egyptians killed.

224 | The first ten amendments to the United States Constitution are:

Article I. Congress shall make no law respecting an establishment of religion, or prohibiting the free exercise thereof; or abridging the freedom of speech, or of the press; or the right of the people peaceably to assemble, and to petition the Government for a redress of grievances.

Article II. A well regulated Militia, being necessary to the security of a free State, the right of the people to keep and bear Arms, shall not be infringed.

Article III. No Soldier shall, in time of peace be quartered in any house, without the consent of the Owner, nor in time of war, but in a manner to be prescribed by law.

Article IV. The right of the people to be secure in their persons, houses, papers, and effects, against unreasonable searches and seizures, shall not be violated, and no Warrants shall issue, but upon probable cause, supported by Oath or affirmation, and particularly describing the place to be searched, and the persons or things to be seized.

Article V. No person shall be held to answer for a capital, or otherwise infamous crime, unless on a presentment or indictment of a Grand Jury, except in cases arising in the land or naval forces, or in the Militia, when in actual service in time of War or public danger; nor shall any person be subject for the same offence to be twice put in jeopardy of life or limb; nor shall be compelled in any criminal case to be a witness against himself, nor be deprived of life, liberty, or property, without due process of law; nor shall private property be taken for public use without just compensation.

Article VI. In all criminal prosecutions, the accused shall enjoy the right to a speedy and public trial, by an impartial jury of the State and district wherein the crime shall have been committed, which district shall have been previously ascertained by law, and to be informed of the nature and cause of the accusation; to be confronted with the witnesses against him; to have compulsory process for obtaining Witnesses in his favor, and to have the assistance of counsel for his defence.

Article VII. In Suits at common law, where the value in controversy shall exceed twenty dollars, the right of trial by jury shall be preserved, and no fact tried by a jury, shall be otherwise reexamined in any Court of the United States, than according to the rules of the common law.

Article VIII. Excessive bail shall not be required, nor excessive fines imposed, nor cruel and unusual punishments inflicted.

Article IX. The enumeration in the Constitution, of certain rights, shall not be construed to deny or disparage others retained by the people.

Article X. The powers not delegated to the United States by the Constitution, nor prohibited by it to the States, are reserved to the States respectively, or to the people.

225 | The ten filmmakers who refused to testify before the House Committee on Un-American Activities in 1947 regarding their Communist party affiliations were producer-director Herbert Biberman, director Edward Dmytryk, producer-writer Adrian Scott, and screenwriters Alvah Bessie, Lester Cole, Ring Lardner, Jr., John Howard Lawson, Albert Maltz, Samuel Ornitz, and Dalton Trumbo.

226 | The ten events that compose the decathlon in the Olympics are the 100-meter dash, broad jump, shot put, high jump, and 400-meter run on the first day; the 110-meter hurdle race, discus throw, pole vault, javelin throw, and 1,500-meter run on the second day.

227 | These are *Variety*'s top ten All-Time Rental Champion Films,* those that have returned the most film rentals to their distributors from release in the United States and Canada. (Film rentals are that portion of box-office ticket-sale grosses remitted by exhibitors to the film's distributor.)

1. *E. T. The Extra-Terrestrial* (1982) $228,618,939
2. *Star Wars* (1977) $193,500,000
3. *Return of the Jedi* (1983) $168,002,414
4. *Batman* (1989) $150,500,000
5. *The Empire Strikes Back* (1980) $141,600,000
6. *Ghostbusters* (1984) $130,211,324
7. *Jaws* (1975) $129,549,325
8. *Raiders of the Lost Ark* (1981) $115,598,000
9. *Indiana Jones and the Last Crusade* (1989) $115,500,000
10. *Indiana Jones and the Temple of Doom* (1984) $109,000,000

---

*As published in the January 24, 1990, issue.

Reprinted with permission of VARIETY INC. VARIETY is a registered trademark of VARIETY INC.

228 | In 1982, *Sight and Sound* invited 122 film critics all over the world to submit their lists of the top ten films of all time. The results were:

1. *Citizen Kane* (1941; Orson Welles)
2. *La Règle du Jeu (The Rules of the Game)* (1939; Jean Renoir)
3. *The Seven Samurai* (1954; Akira Kurosawa)
   Singin' in the Rain (1952; Stanley Donen and Gene Kelly)
4. *8½* (1963; Federico Fellini)
5. *Battleship Potemkin* (1925; Sergei Eisenstein)
6. *L'Avventura* (1960; Michelangelo Antonioni)
   The Magnificent Ambersons (1942; Orson Welles)
   Vertigo (1958; Alfred Hitchcock)
7. *The General* (1926; Buster Keaton and Clyde Bruckman)
   The Searchers (1956; John Ford)

Reprinted by permission of *Sight and Sound.*

229 | These are the top ten TV series of all time, as of the end of the 1988–89 season. Ratings are based on the number of seasons the series was telecast and its audience-size ranking each year.

1. *Gunsmoke* (1955–75)
2. *60 Minutes* (1968–   )
3. *The Red Skelton Show* (1951–71)
4. *Bonanza* (1959–73)
5. *All in the Family/Archie Bunker's Place* (1971–83)
6. *The Ed Sullivan Show/Toast of the Town* (1948–71)
7. *Walt Disney* (1954–   )
8. *The Lucy Show/Here's Lucy** (1962–74)
9. *M*A*S*H* (1972–83)
10. *Dallas* (1978–   )

---

*I Love Lucy (1951–61) ranks fourteenth.

From *The Complete Dictionary to Prime Time Network TV Shows, 1946–Present,* by Tim Brooks and Earle Marsh, updated through 1989.

230 | The ten records that occupied the highest position the longest on *Billboard*'s charts from 1955 to 1988:

TITLE/ARTIST	No. of wks. #1	No. of wks. Top 10
1. "DON'T BE CRUEL/HOUND DOG" Elvis Presley (1956)	11	21
2. "CHERRY PINK AND APPLE BLOSSOM WHITE" Perez Prado (1955)	10	20
3. "SINCERELY" The McGuire Sisters (1955)	10	18
4. "SINGING THE BLUES" Guy Mitchell (1956)	10	17
5. "PHYSICAL" Olivia Newton-John (1981)	10	15
6. "YOU LIGHT UP MY LIFE" Debby Boone (1977)	10	14
7. "MACK THE KNIFE" Bobby Darin (1959)	9	16
8. "ALL SHOOK UP" Elvis Presley (1957)	9	15
9. "BETTE DAVIS EYES" Kim Carnes (1981)	9	14
10. "HEY JUDE" The Beatles (1968)	9	14

231 | Frank W. Benson, Joseph De Camp, Thomas W. Dewing, Childe Hassam, Willard L. Metcalf, Robert Reid, Edward E. Simmons, Edmund C. Tarbell, John Henry Twachtman, and J. Alden Weir made up The Ten, a group of American painters who exhibited together starting in 1898 in order to call attention to their work. When Twachtman died in 1902, William Merritt Chase replaced him.

232 | The colleges in the Big Ten Conference are the universities of Illinois, Iowa, Michigan, Minnesota, and Wisconsin; Michigan State; Ohio State; and Indiana, Northwestern, and Purdue universities.

233 | The members of this college athletic association are the University of California at Berkeley, the University of California at Los Angeles (UCLA), the University of Southern California (USC), the University of Oregon, Oregon State University, Stanford University, the University of Washington, Washington State University, the University of Arizona, and Arizona State University.

234 | The ten provinces are Alberta, British Columbia, Manitoba, New Brunswick, Newfoundland, Nova Scotia, Ontario, Prince Edward Island, Quebec, and Saskatchewan. (The two territories are the Northwest Territories and the Yukon Territory.)

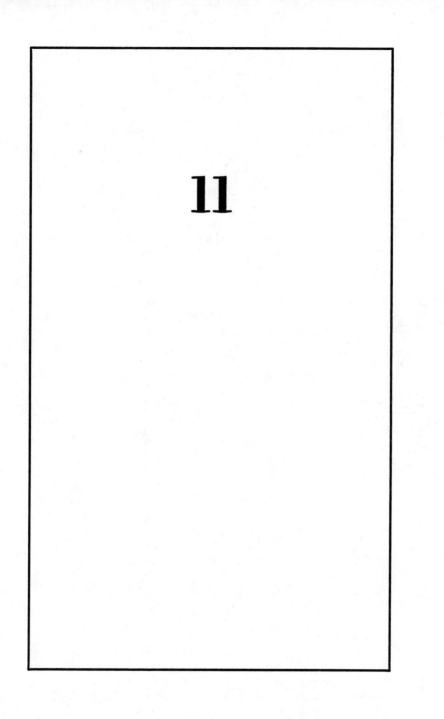

11

235 | The title performers in *Ocean's Eleven* (1960), the quintessential "Rat Pack" movie, were Frank Sinatra, Dean Martin, Sammy Davis, Jr., Peter Lawford, Joey Bishop, Richard Conte, Henry Silva, Norman Fell, Buddy Lester, Clem Harvey, and Richard Benedict.

236 | The eleven states that seceded from the Union in 1860–61 were Alabama, Florida, Georgia, Louisiana, Mississippi, South Carolina, Texas, Arkansas, North Carolina, Tennessee, and Virginia.

12

237 | The twelve original disciples of Jesus were Simon Peter; Andrew; James the son of Zebedee; John his brother; Philip; Bartholomew; Matthew; Thomas; James the son of Alphaeus; Simon the Canaanite, also called Simon Zelotes; Judas the brother of James, also called Thaddaeus; and Judas Iscariot. After Judas Iscariot's betrayal, Matthias was chosen to be the twelfth apostle.

238 | The Twelve Tribes of Israel derived from the twelve sons of Jacob (also known as the twelve patriarchs): Reuben, Simeon, Levi, Judah, Zebulun, Issachar, Dan, Gad, Asher, Naphtali, Joseph, and Benjamin. But when Moses conferred priestly status on the tribe of Levi, the tribe of Joseph was divided into the tribes of Ephraim and Manasseh (his sons) to maintain the number twelve.

239 | 1. We admitted we were powerless over alcohol—that our lives had become unmanageable.
2. Came to believe that a Power greater than ourselves could restore us to sanity.
3. Made a decision to turn our will and our lives over to the care of God *as we understood Him.*
4. Made a searching and fearless moral inventory of ourselves.
5. Admitted to God, to ourselves, and to another human being the exact nature of our wrongs.
6. Were entirely ready to have God remove all these defects of character.
7. Humbly asked Him to remove our shortcomings.

8. Made a list of all persons we had harmed, and became willing to make amends to them all.
9. Made direct amends to such people wherever possible, except when to do so would injure them or others.
10. Continued to take personal inventory and when we were wrong promptly admitted it.
11. Sought through prayer and meditation to improve our conscious contact with God *as we understood Him,* praying only for knowledge of His will for us and the power to carry that out.
12. Having had a spiritual awakening as the result of these steps, we tried to carry this message to alcoholics and to practice these principles in all our affairs.

240 | Belgium, Denmark, France, the Federal Republic of Germany, Greece, Ireland, Italy, Luxembourg, the Netherlands, Portugal, Spain, and the United Kingdom are the twelve members of the European Community, the collective designation of the European Economic Community (the EEC or Common Market), the European Coal and Steel Community, and the European Atomic Energy Community.

241 | First day: A partridge in a pear tree.

Second day: Two turtle doves.

Third day: Three French hens.

Fourth day: Four calling birds. In the English (and presumably the original) version, it's *colly* birds, i.e., blackbirds.

Fifth day: Five gold rings.

Sixth day: Six geese a-laying.

Seventh day: Seven swans a-swimming.

Eighth day: Eight maids a-milking.

Ninth day: From this point on, for some odd reason, the sequence is up for grabs. In some versions, it's nine ladies dancing; in others, nine drummers drumming; in still others, nine pipers piping.

Tenth day: Ten lords a-leaping, or ten pipers piping, or ten drummers drumming.

Eleventh day: Eleven pipers piping, or eleven ladies dancing, or eleven lords a-leaping.

Twelfth day: Twelve drummers drumming, or twelve lords a-leaping, or twelve ladies dancing.

242 In Shiite Islam, the Imāmiyya, literally the "Twelvers," believe in twelve imāms, or leaders of the faith, in a line of succession from Muhammad: Alī, the Prophet's son-in-law; Alī's sons Hasan and Husayn; Alī Zain al-Ābidīn; Muhammad al-Bāqir; Ja'far al-Sādiq; Mūsā al-Kāzim; Alī al-Ridā; Muhammad al-Jawād; Alī al-Hadī; al-Hasan al-'Askarī; and Muhammad al-Muntazar (al-Mahdī).

243 Heracles, the son of Zeus and Alcmena, was driven mad by Hera, Zeus' wife, and murdered his wife and children. In expiation he bound himself to the service of his cousin, Eurystheus, who imposed upon him twelve labors:

1. The slaying of the Nemean lion. Heracles strangled the monster to death and thereafter wore its skin.
2. The slaying of the Lernaean Hydra. The Hydra was a fearsome multiheaded serpent whose heads grew back as soon as they were cut off. After Heracles hacked off the heads, his friend Iolaus burned the stumps with brands, thus preventing the heads from growing back.
3. The capture of the Erymanthian boar. Heracles captured the savage beast that lived on Mount Erymanthus by driving it into a snowfield and trapping it in a net.
4. The capture of the Cerynitian hind, or stag. Heracles chased this golden-horned creature, sacred to Artemis, for a year before capturing it alive.
5. The cleansing of the Augean stables. Heracles was required to clean in one day the stables of Augeas, king of Elis. The stables housed enormous herds of cattle and had never been cleaned before. He accomplished this by diverting the river Alpheus through them.
6. The destruction of the man-eating Stymphalian birds. Heracles drove them out of the woods by means of a bronze rattle, then shot them down with arrows.
7. The capture of the Cretan bull. This savage bull was captured alive and then released.
8. The capture of the horses of Diomedes. King Diomedes' horses were fed on human flesh, and after killing Diomedes Heracles fed his body to the horses, which then became tame.
9. The taking of the girdle of Hippolyte, queen of the Amazons. Because the daughter of Eurystheus

desired the girdle, Heracles sailed to the kingdom of the Amazons to procure it. Hera, disguised as an Amazon, incited a battle between the Amazons and Heracles' followers. The latter won, and Heracles either killed Hippolyte and took the girdle from her or she surrendered it.

10. The seizing of the cattle of Geryon. Heracles journeyed to the far west, where he erected the two pillars of Calpe and Abyla (Pillars of Hercules). On the island of Erytheia he slew the three-bodied giant Geryon, stole his cattle, and returned home, having many more adventures along the way.

11. The stealing of the golden apples of the Hesperides (nymphs of the evening). These apples were kept in a garden at the edge of the world that was guarded by a dragon. Heracles obtained the apples by slaying the dragon and taking them himself, or, alternatively, by sending Atlas for them, holding up the sky in Atlas' place as Atlas did so.

12. The bringing back of Cerberus from the underworld. Heracles descended to Hades, captured Cerberus, the three-headed dog that guarded the gates, brought him to Eurystheus, and then returned him to the underworld.

244 | The twelve months of the French republican calendar, which was adopted in 1793 during the French Revolution and abandoned under the Napoleonic regime in 1805, each contained three periods of ten days (*décades*). The months were Vendémiaire ("vintage month," September 22–October 21), Brumaire (month of "mist" or "fog," October 22–November 20), Frimaire ("frost," November 21–December 20), Nivôse ("snow," December 21–January 19), Pluviôse ("rain," January 20–February 18), Ventôse ("wind," February 19–March 20), Germinal ("seedtime," March 21–April 19), Floréal ("blossom," April 20–May 19), Prairial ("meadow," May 20–June 18), Messidor ("harvest," June 19–July 18), Thermidor ("heat," July 19–August 17), and Fructidor ("fruits," August 18–September 16). At the end of the year there were five supplementary days. (Dates are approximate by a day or two.)

245 | Tishri (September–October of the Gregorian calendar), Marheshvan (October–November), Kislev (November–December), Tevet or Tebet (December–January), Shevat or Shebat (January–February), Adar (February–March), Nisan (March–April), Iyar or Iyyar (April–May), Sivan (May–June), Tammuz (June–July), Av or Ab (July–August), and Elul (August–September). The thirteenth month of the leap year is Adar Sheni or ve-Adar (between Adar and Nisan).

246 | The twelve signs of the Zodiac and the approximate times the sun passes through them (dates vary on many lists by a day or two) are:

Aries (Ram): March 21–April 19

Taurus (Bull): April 20–May 20

Gemini (Twins): May 21–June 21

Cancer (Crab): June 22–July 22

Leo (Lion): July 23–August 22

Virgo (Virgin): August 23–September 22

Libra (Balance): September 23–October 23

Scorpio (Scorpion): October 24–November 21

Sagittarius (Archer): November 22–December 21

Capricorn (Goat): December 22–January 19

Aquarius (Water Bearer): January 20–February 18

Pisces (Fish): February 19–March 20

247 | The title characters in *The Dirty Dozen* (1967) were
Lee Marvin, Charles Bronson, Jim Brown, John
Cassavetes, Telly Savalas, Donald Sutherland, Richard
Jaeckel, Clint Walker, Trini Lopez, Ben Carruthers,
Stuart Cooper, Robert Phillips, and Colin Maitland.
Other well-known actors in the cast were Robert Ryan,
Ernest Borgnine, and Robert Webber.

248 | The twelve paired nerves common to reptiles,
birds, and mammals are the olfactory (I), optic
(II), oculomotor (III), trochlear (IV), trigeminal (V),
abducens (VI), facial (VII), acoustic (VIII), glossophar-
yngeal (IX), vagus (X), accessory (XI), and hypoglossal
(XII).

249 | The Olympian gods were Zeus, Hera, Poseidon,
Athena, Apollo, Artemis, Aphrodite, Hermes,
Demeter, Hephaestus, Ares, and Dionysus. On some
lists Hestia appears instead of Dionysus

250 | The jurors in *12 Angry Men,* Sidney Lumet's 1957
film version of Reginald Rose's television drama,
were Henry Fonda, Lee J. Cobb, Jack Warden, E. G.
Marshall, Ed Begley, Martin Balsam, Jack Klugman,
Robert Webber, George Voskovec, Edward Binns, John
Fiedler, and Joseph Sweeney.

251 | The twelve minor prophets of the Old Testament are Hosea, Joel, Amos, Obadiah, Jonah, Micah, Nahum, Habakkuk, Zephaniah, Haggai, Zechariah, and Malachi.

13

252 | The British colonies that became the original thirteen states of the United States were Massachusetts, New Hampshire, Rhode Island, Connecticut, New York, New Jersey, Pennsylvania, Delaware, Maryland, Virginia, North Carolina, South Carolina, and Georgia.

253 | The thirteen tenets of the Jewish faith according to Maimonides are:

1. There is one God, who created all things.
2. God's unity is absolute; He shares his divinity with no other.
3. God is without material form.
4. God is eternal.
5. God alone is to be worshiped.
6. All the words of the prophets are true.
7. The chief of these prophets is Moses.
8. God's law is the same as that given to Moses.
9. God's law will never be changed, and no other will be given.
10. God is omniscient.
11. God rewards those who obey His commandments and punishes those who transgress.
12. The Messiah will come.
13. The dead shall rise again.

14

254 | The fourteen events of Jesus' Crucifixion, as portrayed in pictures or images that parallel his journey to Calvary, are:

1. Jesus is condemned to death.
2. Jesus is made to carry his cross.
3. Jesus falls for the first time.
4. Jesus meets his mother.
5. Simon of Cyrene is made to bear the cross.
6. Veronica wipes Jesus' face.
7. Jesus falls the second time.
8. The women of Jerusalem weep over Jesus.
9. Jesus falls the third time.
10. Jesus is stripped of his garments.
11. Jesus is nailed to the cross.
12. Jesus dies on the cross.
13. Jesus is taken down from the cross.
14. Jesus' body is laid in the tomb.

255 | President Woodrow Wilson's fourteen proposals for a post–World War I peace settlement, outlined in a speech to Congress on January 8, 1918, were:

1. Open covenants of peace, openly arrived at, after which there shall be no private international understandings of any kind but diplomacy shall proceed always frankly and in the public view.
2. Absolute freedom of navigation upon the seas, outside territorial waters, alike in peace and in war, except as the seas may be closed in whole or in part by international action for the enforcement of international covenants.
3. The removal, so far as possible, of all economic barriers and the establishment of an equality of trade conditions among all the nations consenting

to the peace and associating themselves for its maintenance.

4. Adequate guarantees given and taken that national armaments will be reduced to the lowest point consistent with domestic safety.

5. A free, open-minded, and absolutely impartial adjustment of all colonial claims, based upon a strict observance of the principle that in determining all such questions of sovereignty the interests of the populations concerned must have equal weight with the equitable claims of the government whose title is to be determined.

6. The evacuation of all Russian territory and such a settlement of all questions affecting Russia as will secure the best and freest coöperation of the other nations of the world in obtaining for her an unhampered and unembarrassed opportunity for the independent determination of her own political development and national policy and assure her of a sincere welcome into the society of free nations under institutions of her own choosing; and, more than a welcome, assistance also of every kind that she may need and may herself desire. The treatment accorded Russia by her sister nations in the months to come will be the acid test of their good will, of their comprehension of her needs as distinguished from their own interests, and of their intelligent and unselfish sympathy.

7. Belgium, the whole world will agree, must be evacuated and restored, without any attempt to limit the sovereignty which she enjoys in common with all other free nations. No other single act will serve as this will serve to restore confidence among the nations in the laws which they have themselves set

and determined for the government of their relations with one another. Without this healing act the whole structure and validity of international law is forever impaired.

8. All French territory should be freed and the invaded portions restored, and the wrong done to France by Prussia in 1871 in the matter of Alsace-Lorraine, which has unsettled the peace of the world for nearly fifty years, should be righted, in order that peace may once more be made secure in the interest of all.

9. A readjustment of the frontiers of Italy should be effected along clearly recognizable lines of nationality.

10. The peoples of Austria-Hungary, whose place among the nations we wish to see safeguarded and assured, should be accorded the freest opportunity of autonomous development.

11. Rumania, Serbia, and Montenegro should be evacuated; occupied territories restored; Serbia accorded free and secure access to the sea; and the relations of the several Balkan states to one another determined by friendly counsel along historically established lines of allegiance and nationality; and international guarantees of the political and economic independence and territorial integrity of the several Balkan states should be entered into.

12. The Turkish portions of the present Ottoman Empire should be assured a secure sovereignty, but the other nationalities which are now under Turkish rule should be assured an undoubted security of life and an absolutely unmolested opportunity of autonomous development, and the Dardanelles should be permanently opened as a free passage to

the ships and commerce of all nations under international guarantees.

13. An independent Polish state should be erected which should include the territories inhabited by indisputably Polish populations, which should be assured a free and secure access to the sea, and whose political and economic independence and territorial integrity should be guaranteed by international covenant.

14. A general association of nations must by formed under specific covenants for the purpose of affording mutual guarantees of political independence and territorial integrity to great and small states alike.